Facebook Growth Hacking

How to Correctly Set Up and Maintain Your Facebook Presence and Gain Massive Amounts of Fans

By Jeff Abston

Copyright © 2018 Jeff Abston

All rights reserved.

ISBN: 198634018X

ISBN-13: 978-1986340182

© Copyright 2018 by Jeff Abston - All rights reserved.

This document is geared towards providing exact and reliable information in regard to the topic and issues covered. The publication is sold with the idea that the publisher is not required to render accounting, officially permitted, or otherwise, qualified services. If advice is necessary, legal or professional, a practiced individual in the profession should be ordered.

- From a Declaration of Principles which was accepted and approved equally by a Committee of the American Bar Association and a Committee of Publishers and Associations.

In no way is it legal to reproduce, duplicate, or transmit any part of this document in either electronic means or in printed format. Recording of this publication is strictly prohibited and any storage of this document is not allowed unless with written permission from the publisher. All rights reserved.

The information provided herein is stated to be truthful and consistent, in that any liability, in terms of inattention or otherwise, by any usage or abuse of any policies, processes, or directions contained within is the solitary and utter responsibility of the recipient reader. Under no circumstances will any legal responsibility or blame be held against the publisher for any reparation, damages, or monetary loss due to the information herein, either directly or indirectly.

Respective authors own all copyrights not held by the publisher.

The information herein is offered for informational purposes solely and is universal as such. The presentation of the information is without contract or any type of guarantee or assurance.

Table of Contents

INTRODUCTION 1

A GROWTH HACKER 4

GENERATE MASSIVE TRAFFIC TO YOUR WEBSITE 7

SETTING UP YOUR BUSINESS FOR MASSIVE GROWTH THROUGH FACEBOOK 9

A GUIDE ON HOW TO GROWTH HACK WITH FACEBOOK............ 16

HOW TO GROWTH HACK WITH FACEBOOK ADVERTISING 21

FACEBOOK FAN PAGE STRATEGY 26

SECRETS ON HOW TO GET MASSIVE QUALITY TRAFFIC 30

TIPS TO GET PEOPLE TO JOIN YOUR FACEBOOK FAN PAGE 33

HOW TO INCREASE FACEBOOK LIKES 37

FACEBOOK HACKS THAT WILL SKYROCKET YOUR REACH 49

CONCLUSION 54

INTRODUCTION

Facebook is an active platform for entertainment, news, as well as a social networking place for friends and family. However, the same platform plays an important role for many business owners and marketers in identifying and reaching their target audience as well increasing their sales.

Although the connection between popular entertainment and advertising is a generation old--be it through newspapers, television or radio media--Facebook has suggested more fine-tuned ways of targeting a potential audience. This has brought about a maximization of reach for business owners and marketers.

Humongous numbers of people use Facebook actively every day, thus providing a massive collection of data on the platform. This is an added advantage to many business owners to advertise their brand. However, many marketers still do not know how to take full advantage of Facebook Ads. Here are three advanced and effective ways of using Facebook Ads to better target consumers on the platform.

The most basic way to go about ad targeting is to use keywords properly to create interest, thus creating a solid advertising audience. It is not necessary that your business page fans be your ideal customers. Therefore, instead of using Facebook's extensive

Interest, Keyword, and Demographic options, it is better to target consumers who are more likely to buy the brand's product or service. Tools such as targeting specific age range or specific gender are a good way of targeting, but you can also use other interest groups such as industries, job titles, etc. Take suggestions from Facebook to remove any vague idea and target your ideal customer base.

Facebook's data and algorithms are more powerful than you realize. However, it becomes necessary for business owners to create their own data for audience creation. A source base custom audience list makes it possible for advertisers to reach their target audience. Though a business owner cannot direct an ad towards a specific person, with a custom audience, it is easy to target your customer base. Based on an opt-in email marketing list or tracking pixel on a web page, it is possible to create an audience. Different marketing and advertising techniques can be used for this audience. It is also possible to retarget the visitors who visited your web page in the past, by using the tracking pixel. Though it is not guaranteed that the audience will react to the ad, it is the best way to target people who had shown prior interest in your brand.

It is often easier to target people with similar characteristics. If a specific audience has liked the business page and its content, this lookalike audience feature can be made to gain more fans for the brand page as well as create content engagement. Businesses who use social media to highlight their products specifically profit from this feature.

A GROWTH HACKER

A growth hacker is basically someone with discipline, experience, and willpower when it comes to prioritizing and testing any marketing ideas that come into play. After the testing part, the growth hacker takes his time in data analysis to successfully interpret the end results and make the best marketing tactic to scale further.

Growth hacking is the process by which digital marketers do the exact same thing as mentioned above--researching, testing, interpreting, and scaling all possible marketing channels in order to skyrocket a product, business, or individual on search engines, thus creating a strong link between growth hacking and search engine marketing. People dwelling on these marketing tactics often work together in teams; and along with social media managers, PPC managers, and copywriters, they make results happen!

But truth be told, almost everyone needs to be a growth hacker in their own area of expertise. It has become vital to be capable of and willing to perform tests on your work to see if they'll attract lots of attention. It's pretty main stream that if you're not a growth hacker in today's world, you cannot consider yourself a good marketer at all.

Startups are the ones who rely on growth hackers the most, because they believe in their capabilities of scaling them so high that they will beat almost all of their competitors within a couple of weeks. But that's not always the case, unfortunately. It takes an insane amount of time to completely check every single marketing channel, craft all possible email templates for outreaching to public media outlets, design that landing page perfectly so that the bounce rate drops to a more decent percentage, and optimize every single page for the indexing, which is what search engines specialize in.

Growth hacking is considered as the intersection between marketing and technology, because all those tests mentioned above can be iterated with A/B testing, which is something marketers do together with developers. A/B testing helps a lot when it comes to continuous improvement. Marketers run these tests for as long as these tests get them to that "Aha!" moment. Those moments always lead to rapid customer growth, increases in visits and decreases in the bounce rate, and much more of those goodies for which all marketers aim throughout their careers.

But there is so much more to it than just coming up with good and crazy marketing tactics: we mentioned data analysis as one of the final steps of this (almost) never-ending cycle. Data analysis is crucial for knowing when and how to apply and track the acquisition, engagement, retention, and referral, some of the most important points to track in a visitor's lifecycle. For some, the most important points may be the CTR from all those Google AdWords campaigns, or the average percentage of people who respond to your Facebook posts over the previous week.

GENERATE MASSIVE TRAFFIC TO YOUR WEBSITE

There are many ways people can generate traffic to their website. However, when they open up a website or blog, they do not put time into generating traffic. Therefore, their website or blog does not get results. As a result, they quit. When you own your own website or blog, you have to know the three best ways to generate traffic.

1. Social Networking:

Social Networking is an astonishing way to generate traffic. Social Networking can be an example of twitter, Facebook, etc. However, let's concentrate on Twitter and Facebook. You may know both of these platforms. They are really popular and a great way to communicate.

All you have to do on Twitter is to become popular and gain followers. From then on, you can write tweets about your website or blog. The more followers you have, the better chance to generate massive traffic.

Facebook is mostly a place to communicate with friends and colleagues. Yet, if you want to communicate with random people, you have to open up a fan page. The more people that like your fan page, the more traffic you gain to your website or blog. Just keep in mind, networking with people is a key to a successful website or blog.

2. Video Marketing:

Another great way to generate traffic to your website is by video marketing. An example of video marketing is YouTube. When you have exciting moments and take a video of them, you can put it up on YouTube and share it with the world. Here is a chance for you to make a video about your website or blog and how it can benefit people. Moreover, on the bottom of the video, you can provide the viewers with a link to your site. This is a really way to generate traffic.

3. Article Marketing:

Article marketing is a fascinating way to generate traffic. You simply write an article about what you offer on your site and let people read it. For instance, if you are selling health and fitness products, you write an article that gives people information on how to be healthy. After the article, you then move the reader back to your website with a link. But remember, your product has to be really helpful. If it is, the visitor will buy it.

SETTING UP YOUR BUSINESS FOR MASSIVE GROWTH THROUGH FACEBOOK

One of my favorite tactics when speaking about business growth is asking "social media strategists" to raise their hands. Because there's no such thing as a "social media strategist".

There are business strategists and then there are channel-level tacticians.

- If something changes a lot, then it's a tactic- not a strategy.
- If it's at the channel level, it's a tactic- not a strategy.

You still want your content shared by high authority sites, publications and people. The "hack" is that you get crazy good efficiency when you get results with minimum dosage, which is where these six phases of growth hacking Facebook come into play.

1. DIGITAL PLUMBING

The first phase is "digital plumbing"- meaning your tracking of audience and conversions, mainly via Google Tag Manager. Yes,

Google Tag Manager, even though this is supposed to be about social media.

Social media, properly understood, is actually remarketing— following people around based on what they just did. So web remarketing, smart email marketing, and even direct mail is remarketing.

You need this phase in place to build your audiences and track results. With reliable analytics, you can determine where an additional ounce of effort or dollar in ad spend can work the hardest.

Then there are the next three phases condensed into one acronym: GCT (goals, content, targeting). This is what you must bring to the table as the client. GCT is your business strategy (remember what we said earlier about strategy not being a channel-level thing).

If you're missing any one of these three items (goals, content, or targeting), no amount of Facebook witchcraft will overcome your deficiency. Here's how they apply, broken down:

2. GOALS

The Goals phase containing your story, mission, and goals will determine the key performance metrics that will measure your social investment.

Your story and mission is your WHY- your drive that attracts people to you and aligns them to your brands message.

When determining campaign goals, ask yourself: what are you trying to achieve? Are you:

- Wanting more fans on your Facebook page?
- Driving users to a checkout?
- Collecting emails for a list?
- Raising awareness for an event?

Every campaign has a different goal, so there's no one-size-fits-all strategy that you can apply to everything--each one has it's own requirements and end conditions, so make sure you have your frameworks in place to support your goal.

3. CONTENT

Content is any sort of media (videos, pictures, text, etc) that delivers and supports your message, and is aligned with your Goals. Depending on where your audience is at in the funnel, you'll identify key pieces of content that will nudge them along the funnel until they convert.

Content can exist on your blog, on standalone pages on your site, on your pricing page, or entirely within a Facebook post. It's up to you to come up with the proper strategy on how you structure and distribute your content...

But one thing is for sure, Social Media marketing is content marketing. A Facebook post is simply a (usually) small piece of consumable content placed closer to where your audience likes to hang out: on Facebook.

Thus your goal for any content on Facebook (be it an ad, a traditional post, a video, or even a Facebook note) is really to grab the attention of your prospective customers, and customers, and gently drag them back to your site, where you can capture additional information from them, give them additional information about you, your products and/or services, and, of course, eventually sell them something.

Without a clear content marketing strategy, you really cannot expect significant results. And making content that appeals to the prospective customer and converts them into a buyer rarely happens by accident; it takes a plan.

Design content for various stages of your customer's journey and serve Facebook ads targeting users based on where they are in their journey. Which brings us nicely to the next phase…

4. TARGETING

Within the Targeting phase, you'll define the audience you want to reach. This will be the top few Target Groups that will help you reach your ideal target audience.

Always start narrow with your targeting and expand to encompass larger and larger groups as you scale your campaign. The more specific you start, the better chance that your efforts will pay off. But don't get discouraged if many of your ad groups fail early on; it's been said that 8 out of 10 Facebook ads fail. Your job is to recognize the 2 that succeed and double down on them.

To determine the quality of various target groups, measure their performance against your goals. To do that, you have your plumbing in place with pixels tracking conversions.

Without conversion tracking, you can never properly scale a campaign, because there will be this glaring gap in your data where you "think" you are +ROI, but you can never really be certain. So make sure to connect the dots between your ads and your conversions.

And when targeting past website visitors, there are many different types of retargeting ads that you can consider running on a dollar a day in ad spend or less. Start with something simple like just getting them back to your website, or sending them to your best performing blog post, and test it out as opposed to sending them directly to your sales or pricing page and see which one yields the result you're looking for.

5. AMPLIFICATION

Amplification is paying to boost your content. You see these as sponsored posts or ads on social networks, and they are powerful enough to target down to a single person, or even specific behaviors of your intended audiences.

Once we have established the triage of Goals, Content, and Targeting, you'll create three kinds of ads and amplify the most important pieces of content that will attract the most relevant people and drive engagement.

You'll want to intensify your promotional efforts to the engaged crowd for conversions and place brand content in the newsfeeds of influencers to intercept the media.

Compare the performance of all your posts to determine which are getting the most likes, shares, and comments (LSC) from your audience and use that content, that messaging, or that strategy in your paid ads.

6. OPTIMIZATION

Once you figure out what is working and what isn't, it's time to fine-tune your strategy. My favorite method of optimization is another acronym within the 9 triangles called MAA (Metrics, Analysis, Action).

Get your performance data, analyze the data, and then form a strategy based on your goals– all within a rapid iteration cycle of small, measurable changes every time. The key here is that you have to constantly and repeatedly iterate. Stay in the game.

Use analytics to determine where to put your additional effort or dollar in ad spend. Expand on working audiences, tweak bidding and creatives where necessary, re-allocate budgets and always measure your performance in terms of your Content and Targeting against your Goals to define success.

It's as simple as keeping what performs, and dumping what doesn't.

A GUIDE ON HOW TO GROWTH HACK WITH FACEBOOK

Facebook is the world's biggest social advertising platform, and its Messenger app is now one of the world's most popular apps. Start up or not, you'll want to get a slice of Facebook.

So, what exactly is the best way to engage with this social media? How can growth hackers and early stage business owners make the most of Facebook?

- **Cut through the hype**

Recent algorithmic developments had people predicting the demise of the Facebook page and the steady retreat of its organic reach. Many marketers feel that the platform is making organic posting harder and harder as its ad revenue continues to grow.

Though some of this organic reach hype may be scaremongering, there is definitely a grain of truth to it. The way that people use Facebook is changing, and quite dramatically so. In 2017, most users engaged with Facebook on mobile, and spent a lot of time interacting with videos. As the user evolves, so does the platform.

Here is how not to get too caught up in the reach/ad debate and lose sight of your goals:

Have a theory or hypothesis you want to test? Run some A/B tests to see whether your hunch was right or not. This is the best way to find out whether changes are actually impacting your niche.

Keep constantly listening to your audience, on Facebook and otherwise. Understanding them should help guide your content strategy.

- **Finding meaningful audiences**

The biggest strength of Facebook for a growth hackers is their data serves (which helped save a mill town from dying).

With SO many years of engagement and user data, Facebook is a great place for building and making the most of custom audiences. You can pretty much niche up (or down) as much as you like, and Facebook advertising success is largely determined by audience segmentation.

Don't be too generalist with audience interests—you want niche and targeted audiences for your ads. Run a few targeting tests to see which segmentation strategy works best for you.

Retargeted audiences can also benefit from further segmentation and analysis; don't settle for "blanket" offers and coupons: engage lapsed customers with personalization and emotional marketing.

- **Ad sequencing is the new storytelling**

The more sophisticated the funnel, the more memorable the story.

A proper ad sequence is essential to a well-groomed Facebook ad campaign. Ad sequencing will help you engage customers at the right time with the right ad, and will also considerably strengthen your overall brand presence and brand story.

From retargeting to up-selling, use your Facebook advertising space as a way to up the ante, not simply boost sales figures. Challenge yourself to more exciting ad formats such as videos and carousels to engage users at all stages of the funnel.

On the organic side, sequencing should also factor into your editorial calendar. Make sure your Facebook posts tell a consistent story.

- **Get into Messenger**

Messenger is the place to be. The open rates on messenger apps beat email hands-down, and early adopters of messenger marketing/customer service will see huge engagement rates.

Act fast. Soon enough, Messenger will become saturated with ads and marketing content. Build a chatbot. No really — it's not as hard as you think. Experiment with some of the bigger platforms and see how messenger marketing can help you scale faster.

- **Global from day one**

Facebook connects pretty much everyone in the world. Brands on Facebook need to take advantage of the platform's global reach to grow faster. With the advance of modern logistics and dropshipping, there is no reason not to start servicing international customers from day one.

Think big with ads. Use a tool like AdEspresso to help you scale and automate your Facebook ads. (Bonus—it hooks up with Instagram too).

Multilingual ads are a great way to really speak to your target audience, but don't go for straight translation—opt for cultural transcreation instead. It will make your ads much more compelling. Same goes for organic content—get access to local and cultural insights so that your posts literally "speak" their language.

- **Building a community**

Facebook is a great place for building an online community, whether it's one that's chiefly organic or advertising based. Adopt a community management attitude instead of a broadcasting one.

You will need to be very good at community management problem-solving: a poorly timed or misjudged update will send your Facebook reactions and comments into a tailspin. Spend time investigating customer and buyer avatars before diving in, and be open and honest about any shortcomings in customer service or experience.

At the same time, if you have a story that goes right to the heart of a community issue or you have a brilliant opportunity to news jack, dive right in. Being the first to market with an angle will give you the edge, as long as you haven't misjudged the community reaction.

- **Multichannel Facebook**

The best way to use Facebook is to integrate it with the rest of your marketing—and beyond. Be constantly on the lookout for ways to repurpose and recycle content, and don't forget to use insights from marketing and customer service data to help you win at Facebook.

Data visualization tools can help busy teams decipher complex data quickly. Take advantage of integrated data platforms to help you deliver the best Facebook experience.

Recognize Facebook's role as a customer service and customer experience channel—not just a marketing one. With the launch of Facebook Workplace, it's already making in-roads into internal processes and HR, too. Make sure you're making the most of the platform with a 360-degree approach.

HOW TO GROWTH HACK WITH FACEBOOK ADVERTISING

Understanding the ruthless Facebook newsfeed!

Ads are actually fighting for visibility on the newsfeed. If you are targeting a specific audience with YXZ interest, XYZ behaviors and XYZ demographic, this chunk with more or less exactly the same interests, behavior and demographics are being targeted by thousands of other advertisers. An advertiser should know the process of broad targeting.

This is how auction and delivery work. When a person goes to his/her newsfeed. Facebook looks at all the ads targeting him/her, ranks the ads based on an effective bid and selects the top effective bid, as represented by this formula.

Effective= advertiser bid x ecvr + F(likes, x-outs, and so on)

Facebook optimizes delivery for actions advertisers care about. However, advertisers can't always make an accurate bid for a target audience with CPM or CPC because they don't know the probability of a person converting against an objective. The only solution for this by Facebook is conversion optimized bidding which estimates the value of an impression for an advertiser by predicting the likelihood that someone will convert against a given action using probabilistic modeling.

Custom Audiences Techniques

1. List the Facebook groups that are similar to your niche and use a tool like growthers.io/grouply to extract member data from a Facebook group, i.e., name, company name and email.

2. After getting the basic information, use Toofr to get their work emails or leadIQ for gmail addresses and add it to your custom audiences. However, keep in mind that Facebook's terms of service require custom audiences to opt in, so play by the rules or put on your gray hat and cross your fingers.

3. Another way is to laser target a single person's newsfeed to get mentions. This is usually done for the higher authority people likethe chief editor of The Next Web or Mashable or business insider, etc. Even if you don't know your target's email address, you can try the most common corporate email patterns such as dave.paul@company.com or dpaul@company.com and get the gmail from LeadIQ. Experiment with a few of these or head to the company website and dig more into the contact information.

Targeting Techniques

1. Use 3-tiered targeting strategy, allot a higher budget for the audience likely to convert, i.e., 1% lookalike based on your most valuable audience.

2. Target the audience with a past purchase record with a bit lower budget than the first and exclude the first tier from it.

3. A tiny fraction of the budget is for 3% to 5% lookalike audiences.

Creative & Relevance Techniques

Keep an eye on the relevance score to see how well connected an ad creative is to a target market. Monitor the score closely and adjust the creative or target audience when needed.

Ad Hack

Try the new link ad format and test it through the Facebook sharing debugger tool.

Photo link ad works as a trigger to boost your conversions; this ad will just look like a native picture but upon tapping it will take you to the landing page instead of opening up an enhanced picture. This ad hack is done with the help of Facebook's Open Graph Meta Tags and by using those tags, one can tell Facebook which image to show as a preview for the link.

Implementation

This code should be added to a new file in your website and needs to be edited through three different options as mentioned below.

```
<!doctype html>
<html lang="en">
<head>

<!--Main Meta Tags -->
 <meta charset="utf-8" />
 <title>PAGE TITLE</title>
 <meta name="description" content="PAGE TITLE" />

 <meta property="og:site_name" content="PAGE TITLE">
 <meta property="og:url" content="IMAGE URL">
 <meta property="og:title" content="PAGE TITLE">
 <meta property="og:description" content="PAGE TITLE">
 <meta property="og:type" content="video.other">
 <meta property="og:image" content="IMAGE URL">
 <meta property="og:image:width" content="800">
 <meta property="og:image:height" content="800">

</head>
<body>
<meta http-equiv="refresh" content="0;URL='WEBSITE URL'" />
</body>
</html>
```

The aforementioned HTML code should be added to a new file on your website that you want to use as a destination. Later on this link will be shared on your Facebook page to generate the large photo link ad image. You will need to edit your code in three different ways.

Page Title: Insert a decent tittle for the link you are advertising; this won't be shown on Facebook but its better to insert something relevant.

Image URL: Upload 800×800 image file to the same site where the aforementioned code will be copy and pasted. This image URL will be displayed on Facebook.

Website URL: The website destination/URL that will opened after clicking on the image URL displayed on Facebook.

Once you are done editing with the code, check it through the Facebook Sharing Debugger Tool to verify the image dimension and how it will look on your page.

Happy Advertising!

FACEBOOK FAN PAGE STRATEGY

Facebook is a social networking utility that links people influenced by networks. Networks can be determined by a wide variety of things and are based on the information you provide within your user profile. Once you sign up for Facebook, it is possible to connect with a multitude of networks and meet numerous people who are similar to you. A lot of people have used Facebook to meet lots of wonderful people; and if you are interested in using the Internet to meet people, then Facebook might be the web page you're interested in.

Businesses that make use of Facebook and Facebook fan pages to advertise their company to potential clients can easily increase product sales.

We often hear that the concept of using Facebook to gain business is lost on realtors and the opportunity is brushed off as pointless. At this time, Facebook has collected more than five hundred million active users and that number is increasing day by day. The number of fan pages on Facebook is also growing rapidly.

Since social networking channels attract a great deal of regular interest by Internet users, social media marketing platforms happens to be an excellent for entrepreneurs to generate interest and target traffic. Facebook is the very first and the primary social networking group that is extremely effective for establishing business globally.

If you're just like the majority of business people, you would like as many people as possible to locate you on the Internet. If you just create a user profile with your company name, you're certainly not capitalizing on your publicity. Creating a Facebook fan page will give your company the boost you have been wanting.

Build your page with a custom landing tab or have someone do it for you.

Engage with your audience.

Engage with your community.

As soon as you have your fan page all set, you can easily think of expanding your group of fans tremendously utilizing Facebook Ads. Some of our customers have added many new, targeted, engaged followers to their pages by implementing our strategic marketing and advertising techniques.

It's fascinating, but it will not materialize until you have a fan page of your very own.

In case you have your own organization, you most likely realize by now that, although your company is a real bricks-and-mortar business (for instance, a hardware shop or a sport shoe store), setting up a well-known and well-branded on-line presence has become the most crucial thing to do.

Below are some Facebook fan page techniques that you ought to be using right now to create your brand name and attract extra followers!

To begin with, you must understand that in regard to social networking, one of the top rules is to join as well as become likeable!!

Should your Facebook fan page not reveal the type of feeling your audience is seeking, they most likely will not stay for long!

Update Your Facebook fan page regularly. Another essential Facebook fan page strategy is to be certain to maintain your page with appropriate and useful information, and tips or reports about your particular company or retail store.

Keep your Facebook fan page social and ensure it is interactive. This is probably one of the most challenging tasks, but know that one of the keys to staying interactive is to bear in mind that Facebook is a Social Media platform. It is about hooking up, being societal and cultivating interactions. Ultimately, it truly does not make any difference how fancy or amazing your fan page is if you are not utilizing it to genuinely talk with your friends and followers.

Load it with unique and related contents. This definitely does not need to be related to your products and solutions, but it surely could be anything that provides great value to your enthusiasts.

Facebook Internet marketing is massive and it is simply becoming larger. It can be predicted that over 350 million people are active on Facebook and knowthat each user consumes about fifty-five minutes every day on the platform. By making use of Facebook fan pages, it is possible to grow your prospects and interact with members of your industry who probably are not exposed to your additional advertising and marketing strategies.

SECRETS ON HOW TO GET MASSIVE QUALITY TRAFFIC

We have learned that there are highly effective, secret strategies that will direct traffic to your site and common mistakes that run traffic the other way. You want to use specific techniques that have been researched and proven effective for generating traffic and leads.

Use the following suggestions as a check list to see where you can make improvements to your traffic flow.

USE AN EMAIL LIST

You can get quality leads and massive traffic to add to your list of contacts. This can be family and friends, peers, former classmates, etc. But massive leads are generated when you use the Internet as your marketing playground and not just as a local neighborhood business. Use Google (FREE) Contact Manager to keep track of your contacts or a (PAID) service like AWeber that will send out automated emails and make your marketing much simpler. Create your campaign and begin delivering value and content straight to your prospects' inbox.

CREATE ARTICLES WITH GREAT LINKS

Once you begin to write posts, blogs and comments, you will need to direct prospects to a great place where they can receive free offers and plenty of valuable information. Prospects are looking for direction and enjoy searching sites for bits of value. Design your site properly and make sure the links are not broken. We recommend that you write your article, add a video or image, use links that keep readers engaged and looped in your content. Post these articles in related groups, forums and sites to gain more visibility. Remember to direct traffic to your blog or website.

PURCHASE PPC ADS and/or NEWSPAPER ADS

Network Marketing is about marketing your business and brand to others. There are plenty of ways to market for FREE or on a budget and still get great results. Many leaders have spent thousands upon thousands of dollars learning new strategies, tips and resources that benefit their business. When combining Digital and Traditional Media Marketing, you must realize that a combination of techniques can be an explosive way to get more quality leads and generate massive traffic to your site.

USE YOUR FACEBOOK FAN PAGE and GROUPS

You will generate more leads and traffic by using Facebook as a lead generator. Do not conduct marketing business on your Facebook profile page, but instead create one or more Facebook fan pages specifically related to the content that you want to share. Make comments, reply, engage and report on issues related to your niche. Prospects will be attracted and want more information. These are highly effective social media secrets to use for marketing on Facebook. Your Facebook profile is meant to be for friends, not necessarily customers.

PLEASE SHARE THE CONTENT

Social Media is based on sharing content with others in your communities. Since you put so much time and energy into your content development, you want to make sure that the information gets shared. It is important to ask your fans, friends and followers to share your content. Make certain you have installed the social media icon buttons on your site to make it easier.

SUBMIT A PRESS RELEASE

When you have an event, new product release, updates or anything newsworthy, then you should submit a press release to let the public know. Creating a press release is simple and should be submitted with every campaign launch to announce new products and services.

USE VIDEOS and IMAGES

Creating visually attractive sights can hold visitors' attention longer than a site without images and video. You want visitors to feel at home and let them see a demonstration of the product or service. Use YouTube to add videos, create annotations and notes within a video.

TIPS TO GET PEOPLE TO JOIN YOUR FACEBOOK FAN PAGE

With its new tagging ability, Facebook has made its site a whole lot more appealing for small business owners. They have the ability to seek out the people talking about them, and users can get their voices heard, knowing businesses will check to see who has tagged them. But before either party can take advantage of Facebook's new feature, you first must get your customers to opt into the relationship. You have to give them a reason to friend your Facebook fan page, and that's not always easy.

I've written in the past about how to create a Facebook fan page – how to set it up, what to put on it, how to make it look and feel like your brand. But how do you get people to actually want to join the page? How do you combat brand fatigue and take them from a passive observer to a full-blown brand evangelist?

Make People Feel Part of Something

Think back to high school. You joined cliques for survival and to help you feel liked, respected, wanted, etc. You joined because you were made to feel like you were missing out if you weren't part of the group. Social networking works the same way.

It's very easy to be passive on Facebook. If you want someone to take that step and openly associate themselves with your brand, you need to make them feel like they're missing out by NOT being part of your community. You create this by making your community sound and feel 100x times larger than it actually is (unless you're purposely trying to seem small and elite). You fake it until you make it.

Make tagging part of your fans daily interaction with you. Make a game out of it so you're always showing up on their wall (with a link to your fan page) and they're always showing up on your page. Doing this helps spread your brand, it keeps you top of mind, and it makes people curious as to why they're seeing you all over the place. I mean, how else do you get people to become fans of tarantulas?

Appeal to Core Members

Every group has a core bunch, a handful of folks responsible for change, leading things, getting everyone excited and spreading the company message. Reach out to these folks and get them involved in talking about your fan page.

Create your promotional army by hand selecting the major players, sending messages thanking them for their support, and then telling them you need their help. Make them feel important and on the cutting edge of whatever you're doing. Get them to always be talking about you and tagging your places. These actions will increase your trust, build your credibility and give you social proof. These connectors are usually the ones with very large social networks on sites like Twitter or Facebook. Ask them to use Facebook's Suggest feature to "suggest" that their friends fan your page. When the request comes from them, it's harder for others to decline, and it just reinforces that "inside joke".

Offer Exclusive Content

Facebook is much more intimate than other social media sites. Users are less likely to invite strangers into their networks and are wary of brands. If you want their attention, you have to give them something of value for their effort.

The most popular way of doing this seems to be through Facebook-specific coupons or special offers. Friday's is offering free hamburgers, Victoria Secrets gives away free undies, Sears gives coupons and gift cards, etc. Other brands give away exclusive content via video, photos, applications, advanced notice of events, or even just real interaction with other members. Figure out what your customers crave and then give it to them.

Make Your Fan Page Their Forum

No one wants to join a group where they have no voice. They want to interact with the brands they love and feel like they're being listened to. Once of the best ways to get people to fan your page is to use it as a forum where you ask and listen to customer advice. Let your members lead by turning your fan page into a place where users can express themselves, talk about what they don't like, and things they'd like to see you do in the future. If you have an upcoming campaign or product you're working on, create a

Facebook focus group that encourages people to offer their input. If word gets out that your Facebook Fan page is where you go to crowdsource your ideas, people are going to want to be a part of it. Make your fan page the place where your customers can go to get heard.

Facebook fan pages have always been a valuable way to build a community and learn about your audience. However, now they're also a great way to get users to spread the word about your brand to their friends with the use of tags. Give them a reason to join your fan page. Make it exciting and worth their time. And then encourage them to talk about and tag you, and you will increase the number of eyeballs interacting with you online.

HOW TO INCREASE FACEBOOK LIKES

STRATEGIES, IDEAS & EXAMPLES

These methods apply to both advanced users and newcomers.

1. Facebook contests

Facebook contests are the easiest way to get people excited and draw new users in as fans. The lure of a big prize (one that's relevant to your specific target market) makes it an easy ask for your target customers to also "like" your page and become a fan.

How does a contest get people to "like" your Facebook page and become a fan?

Many people think that without the like-gating feature (deprecated in 2015), contests are no longer useful in generating likes, but that's not true. A contest still engages users, educates them on your brand, and makes them want to gain access to win more valuable prizes down the road. The fact that a user is on your page shows they are interested in your brand. If they are willing to go through the effort of filling out a form, they're someone you're going to want to build a relationship with.

A "like" popup is our solution to the recent extinction of like-gating. It involves a simple popup appearing on the page when a user arrives at the contest tab of your Facebook page. The popup politely asks users to "like" your page so that they can stay connected in the future. It's no longer a requirement of entering a contest, but if users are genuinely interested in your brand, it will be an easy decision to say yes.

2. Coupons

Coupons are a great (and ever-green) promotion sure to increase Facebook likes. Something small like a 10% off coupon gives people an incentive to buy while keeping your margins (relatively) intact. The optimal way to use coupons is to have them require an action to access them (one that doesn't require much work).

A good coupon app makes it easy for you to create your own coupon directly on Facebook. Having a coupon on Facebook makes it super easy to share, as many third parties (yup, like Wishpond) enable you to select the option to auto post to participants' walls. That is, when someone participates to get your coupon code, a post is shown on their Facebook wall, inviting their friends to take part in your coupon offering too.

Just like with the Facebook Contest App mentioned in the previous section, you can add a "like" popup to your coupon, as seen in the example below.

One easy way to drive traffic to your coupon with your "like" popup is to add a call-to-action in the header of your website. Promoting your coupon on your website is a great idea as website visitors are obviously interested in purchasing from you, so a free coupon will be very enticing to them. As they're already showing interest in your business, they are the perfect people to "like" your page and engage with it.

3. EBook "like" popups

Sometimes educational content is a better incentive for a "like" than a discount offer or prize, depending on your industry or target market. For B2B companies especially, providing free written content such as ebooks and whitepapers can drive tons of new fans and customers.

Many ebooks have a download landing page housed on a website that includes a form you must fill out to access the ebook. By housing the ebook download inside a tab on your Facebook page, you can increase your Facebook likes with a "like" popup. If they're interested in downloading your ebook, chances are they're interested in your business and industry posts in the future.

Hosting your ebook directly on your page helps to improve the conversion rate of your Facebook ads. Studies have shown that Facebook ads that link to pages within Facebook result in a higher conversion rate than those that link to pages outside of the platform. This is because visitors to your page see a Facebook like as less invasive than their personal information or email address.

4. Facebook Ads

Facebook ads are the easiest way to increase your valuable Facebook likes. Why? Because you're guaranteed visibility of your brand to a highly-targeted audience. A Facebook ad allows you to target really specifically, ensuring that only your target demographics see it.

One key thing to remember is that Facebook ads are not the same as Google Ads. This is because your Google ad appears when a person is actively searching for your keywords. They are more likely to want to know about your specific offering at that specific time, thus eliciting a click on what is most relevant for their search (the ad).

This isn't the case for Facebook Ads

A Facebook ad appears while a person is just browsing around on their newsfeed, so they most likely won't have an intent to purchase your products at that time. This means you need to provide an incentive to drive clicks on your Facebook ads. I've found the most success comes from using images of people. Studies have shown that an image of a person (particularly a smiling woman) is more eye-catching and converts better than anything else. It's more subtle than a big red arrow, and gets a higher click-through rate.

5. Add a "Like" button or box to your blog

A great strategy for capturing visitors on your blog in a fairly non-invasive way is to get them to like your Facebook page. Many people are averse to signing up for emails due to spam, so a like can be an easy alternative.

To help with conversions, make liking easy for them. Don't make visitors go to your Facebook page first to like you by only providing a link to your page. Allow them to like your page right there from your blog using one of Facebook's social plugins, such as the

Facebook Page Plugin or a Like Button. Making it a single step versus a two-step process will dramatically increase your conversion rate on this simple action.

6. Add a "Like" button to your website's header

Having a Like Button in the top-right or left corner of your website is an easy way to drive new likes over time. For a number of clients, this has been a constant driver of new likes every day. It won't get you a ton all at once, but having it there doesn't hurt anything, and over time those Facebook likes add up.

I recommend adding a Like Button to your header in an easy-to-see position with a simple call-to-action, such as "like us to hear about Facebook-exclusive contests and deals." This allows you to keep it up in perpetuity and not have to worry about updating it every week or two. It will also keep from conflicting with any contests or coupons you promote on your website.

7. Video like popups

Behind-the-scenes, interviews and live event videos are a great incentive to get new Facebook Likes. Just like ebooks, coupons and contests, you can place a "like" popup straight over top of these videos to capture new fans. But these can't just be any videos. These need to be first-time, behind-the-scenes exclusives that you can't find anywhere else. Here are a few examples that make for great exclusives:

Videos from backstage at events

Exclusive video webinars with high-profile influencers

Exclusive how-to guides for your product or service

Why does the content need to be so special?

People can watch videos anywhere, so these need to be particularly interesting in order to earn the Facebook like you're asking for. By engaging potential fans with something new and exciting, they're much more likely to say yes and want to see more in the future.

8. Fill out your about page

Your Facebook profile can often be the first thing people see about your business - it ranks high through SEO and can often be a better source of information than your own website.

Make it easy for readers who visit your Facebook page (and increase Facebook likes) to learn about your business by filling out your about page. Include your opening hours, location and contact information, and a short blurb of information about your business.

Showing people that your Facebook profile is a reliable source of information about your business is a short and simple way to increase Facebook likes.

9. Optimize post times

Facebook's new algorithm has made it hard enough for businesses to find success on Facebook. Find the times (based on your target market) that people are most likely to see and engage with your Facebook posts to maximize your reach and increase likes.

Studies have found that it's best to post on Facebook around 9 a.m., and from 1 to 4 p.m. You know the feeling -- you check Facebook when you first get to work, and again when the day starts to drag on in the afternoon. That being said, weekend posts also do quite well.

It's hard to find the exact best times for your business, but understanding your target market to optimize your Facebook post timing can be key to Facebook success.

10. Post "how-to"s

People appreciate high-value content, and a great example is content that helps them learn something. One way to increase Facebook likes is to post a "how-to" video, showing people how to use your products in new or creative ways.

11. Use Facebook Live

Using Facebook Live to host a Q&A or preview a new product is video with a kick. It's especially engaging because people can react and interact in real-time with your business. Answer viewer questions live "on-air", and make sure you give your fans a heads up (on Facebook and other social platforms) so your attendance is as high as possible

Hosting interesting and engaging Live sessions is an awesome way to show fans the personality behind your business (and increase Facebook likes), while providing them with content that they'll want more of. To make sure they don't miss your next Live event, they'll like your page.

12. Post discounts and promotions

Other than coupons you can use Facebook as a platform to share sales promotions and discounts. Post them with an image (generally more engaging) and a CTA to like your page for the latest promotions.

As you can see in this post from H&M, people wanting 20% off from H&M need to show that they like the H&M page on Facebook - it's a sure way to increase Facebook likes.

13. Promote your page to your email list

Put the list you've been building through lead generation tactics and promotions by sending out a newsletter asking them to like your Facebook page. Make sure they know you'll be sharing the latest deals, content, and promotions to increase Facebook likes.

Something else you can do is append a CTA to the end of each of your email newsletters to like your Facebook page. This doesn't come off as overly promotional (like the previous suggestion might)

14. Add a "like" button to thank you pages

Add prompts and CTAs to like your Facebook page on the thank you pages of your landing pages and popups. People that have already converted on one of your campaigns are more apt to like your Facebook page. This is especially true if they've just entered a contest, as they'll want to follow your social media platforms to see if they've won.

15. Add an exit popup to your website

Add an exit popup with a prompt to like your Facebook page to the pages on your website to direct traffic from your website to your social platforms. Though you might think this is a similar strategy to adding a Like Button to your header or sidebar, adding a popup prompt helps put your page front and center.

16. Get customers to review your business

As mentioned previously, your Facebook profile is often the first point of contact for people who are researching your business. Getting customers to review your business helps establish credibility and convinces new visitors of your business' benefits. Having a slew of good reviews shows customers you're the real deal, and can help increase Facebook likes in the process.

17. Offer customer support on your page

Responding to comments and messages on Facebook from customers with support questions can be a great way to increase Facebook likes. Doing this shows other visitors that you're helpful, your page is active, and that you're using social media as a platform to genuinely connect with your customers. Customers who have received good support, or who may need it in the future, will probably like your page.

18. Partner with influencers

Influencer marketing is a huge part of social media. Connecting with influential figures within your industry to share posts on both your Facebook profiles can help boost your reach to access additional portions of your target market and increase Facebook likes. This also helps create social proof. If influencers support your business, you can bet their fans will be likely to do so as well.

19. Capitalize on trending topics

Posting creative content to capitalize on trending news can help push immediate engagement. Posting content that's relevant to the latest news (e.g. the latest presidential election or award show) is shareable. It's topical -- people are interested in these topics, meaning they're more likely to share and engage with it. Just make sure your posts are at least somewhat relevant to your product.

20. Share user-generated content

Show fans and followers you care about them by sharing the content they post about your products or business. This is a great way to fill out your content calendar, and it encourages other fans to post more content related to your products. More content coming from fans will help spread the name of your business to others in your target market and increase Facebook likes.

21. Give fans a look behind the scenes

Social media is the perfect place to show fans a deeper and less polished look into your business. Show your followers things like your office culture or the making of a new product. This type of content might not drive sales, but it's definitely engaging -- and that means more likes for your page.

22. Share infographics

I love infographics because they make otherwise boring data interesting -- they're effective at condensing information in a way that's digestible and shareable. Posting awesome infographics with information about the latest industry trends or products means more people sharing your content. That's guaranteed to increase Facebook likes!

23. Use Facebook Insights

Taking advantage of Facebook Insights can help you connect better with your customers. Understanding the people who like your page, and the content that best resonates with them, will help you shape your content strategy in the future, meaning you can optimize engagement.

24. Schedule your Facebook posts

I know first-hand how tough it can be to maintain a consistent queue of content for your Facebook page. Thankfully, tools like Buffer make it easy to schedule content days - even weeks – in advance so you don't need to worry about it. Take some time every few days to schedule posts (at optimal times) to go out to your fans, showing them that your page is consistently active and full of great content.

25. Use video

Though text posts and photos are great, trying your best to share different forms of content - like video - can help engage current and future fans. Post creative videos, like behind-the-scenes videos or "making of" video, and you'll be sure to drive engagement and increase Facebook likes.

26. Promote your page in-store

Sometimes, we're too preoccupied with promoting our digital platforms on other digital platforms. One of the best ways to increase Facebook likes is to promote your page URL in your store, on a poster or on receipts - any kind of signage will work! I'd recommend giving people a discount for liking your page, too, as this helps incentivize them to act.

27. Promote your posts

Due to the current Facebook algorithm, it can be tough to reach fans organically with the content you post. Use the Facebook Ads tool to promote posts to people in your target who might be interested. This can increase Facebook likes more than simply promoting your page itself, as your content is likely to be a larger "draw" that can help pull in user attention.

FACEBOOK HACKS THAT WILL SKYROCKET YOUR REACH

Lately, all the rage has been about Facebook ads and how to use the to get click from Facebook on the cheap. But the fact is that you can still get awesome results with Facebook for FREE if you know what you're doing.

1. Seed Your Social Proof

Start by joining groups that relevant to your niche.

Type in some keywords into graph search and you should be able to find several relevant groups to join. Starting your own group is a good idea as well.

Once you are a member of a few relevant groups you should get the ball rolling when you post new content by sharing it to a few groups.

I have observed that people are much faster to like and share a post if it has already been shared.

Share your post after you post it and your reach will benefit from the added group exposure, plus the added social proof.

2. Add a URL After Your Share is Approved

When sharing your post to groups (image and text posts work best for sharing), if it contains a URL, your chances of having the post approved decrease.

What you can do to get around this is to wait until your post is approved and then edit your post and add a link.

Holding off a few minutes before adding a link to your image or post can help you get your first few likes and shares faster since people will see it as a pure value post rather than link bait.

3. Promote Your Link in the Comments

Personally I have found my image posts outperform my pure text posts, but this strategy can be a good workaround for those people who find that their text posts outperform their link and image posts.

The strategy here is to post an all text status update and then include the link you are promoting as the first comment.

4. Upload Videos Directly to Facebook

You might have noticed that videos uploaded directly to Facebook automatically play when someone scrolls by them in the newsfeed. This will get more people watching your videos and will lead to more engagement and reach.

5. Be Brief

Brevity is the soul of wit. ~Shakespeare

Posts with 80 characters or less get 66% more engagement.

6. Hack Your About Section

Include a link within your about section to get more people clicking through to your site.

Using this strategy, it is possible to include two clickable links in your about section and I recommend you implement this even if the two links you are promoting are the same.

The about section is the closest thing in your page sidebar that you have the ability to optimize.

7. Optimize Your Cover Photo

Your cover photo is the most visible part of your page, so make the most of it by featuring a graphic, link and call to action.

For best results, feature a lead magnet (free gift) in your cover photo and make the link to a landing page where they can go to enter their name and email in exchange for the gift.

8. Schedule Posts Ahead of Time

Set aside time at least once a week to schedule content to ensure that you have content ready to go every day of the week.

For maximum reach I recommend scheduling posts from directly within your Facebook page.

Facebook wants you to use Facebook rather than third party apps and they reward your use of their platform with greater reach for native posts.

9. Optimize for Peak Posting Time

The peak posting time is generally from 1-3pm, but every audience is unique so check your insights as this will reveal the peak posting time for your page.

10. Fangate Premium Content

Use fan only content to cause more people to "like" your page.

Of course more Facebook likes will lead to a greater Facebook reach.

11. Use Calls to Action With Engagement Keywords

Including calls to action -- like, share, and comment -- can double your engagement and will get more people taking these actions.

12. Avoid Short URL's

People often mistrust short links since they are essentially redirects that could go anywhere.

To avoid the decreased reach from these links, always use the direct link to the web page you are sharing so more people will trust the link, engage with your post, and click through.

13. Manually Upload Your Photos

Facebook wants you to spend as much time as possible on Facebook so they give greater exposure to pictures uploaded directly to Facebook, rather than from a third party app. Manually upload your photos to give your image posts the best reach possible.

14. Don't Bleed the Feed

Post 1 or 2 times a day. A massive audience posting more than this is understandable, but for the vast majority of pages one or two posts a day will do the trick.

If you have the urge to post more, schedule those posts for the future to ensure you have a steady stream of content flowing for your fans.

15. Use Facebook to Grow Your Email List

Email marketing is a ridiculously powerful channel, so use your Facebook page to build your email list. You can then use email marketing to extend your reach by linking to posts you make on Facebook in the emails you send.

CONCLUSION

You must systematically go through the above content for setting up and running a Facebook campaign in order to prepare the channel for massive growth. Go out of order and you'll have problems – just like a cake missing an ingredient or baked for a random amount of time at a random temperature.

"Growth hacking" on Facebook is based on the same principles as old-fashioned PR, content marketing, word-of-mouth marketing, SEO, one-to-one marketing, or whatever you want to call it.

Why? Because we're trying to get high-authority people to spread our message.

And the content, plus our network, has to be pretty good to convince these trusted peers to share it.

The result is that you get links in high authority places (SEO), more media mentions (PR), and a lot of legit retweets (social media marketing).

Now, what's super cool about Facebook tactically, provided you have the strategic elements in place, is that you can get crazy good results for only a dollar a day.

Why a dollar? Because if you can micro-target exactly who you want to reach (instead of shotgun blasting the planet), then hitting the 200-300 most relevant people with your high quality message is sufficient.

The "influence the influencer" approach is designed to truly provide value (not sales literature) to people who have large audiences such that they'll share it.

You don't have to be a programmer or fantastic public speaker, nor do you have to have much money (a dollar a day- can you spare that?). Use the "dollar a day" technique to get your next job, impress your spouse, wreak havoc on competitors, or get your consumer complaint resolved nearly instantly.

What makes this a hack is that you need only start with one simple goal, one piece of content, and one dollar a day. Then you can layer on as you start to see results.

You don't need to buy fancy software, hire a social media guru, or sign up for a "secret" course. None of these can supply you with your goals, content, and targeting. Getting these items right is how you get crazy results on Facebook, which you can copy over to Google, Twitter, YouTube, LinkedIn, and other channels.

www.ingramcontent.com/pod-product-compliance
Lightning Source LLC
Chambersburg PA
CBHW030051230526
45471CB00003B/1047